CHILD

TEENAGER

KU-167-168

Cat

MENACING –TOO MUCH OF AN EFFORT

SPRAY PAINT

£6.99

Printed and Published in Great Britain by D.C. THOMSON & CO., LTD.,185 Fleet Street, London EC4A 2HS.© D.C. THOMSON & CO., LTD., 2005.   ISBN 1 84535 0464

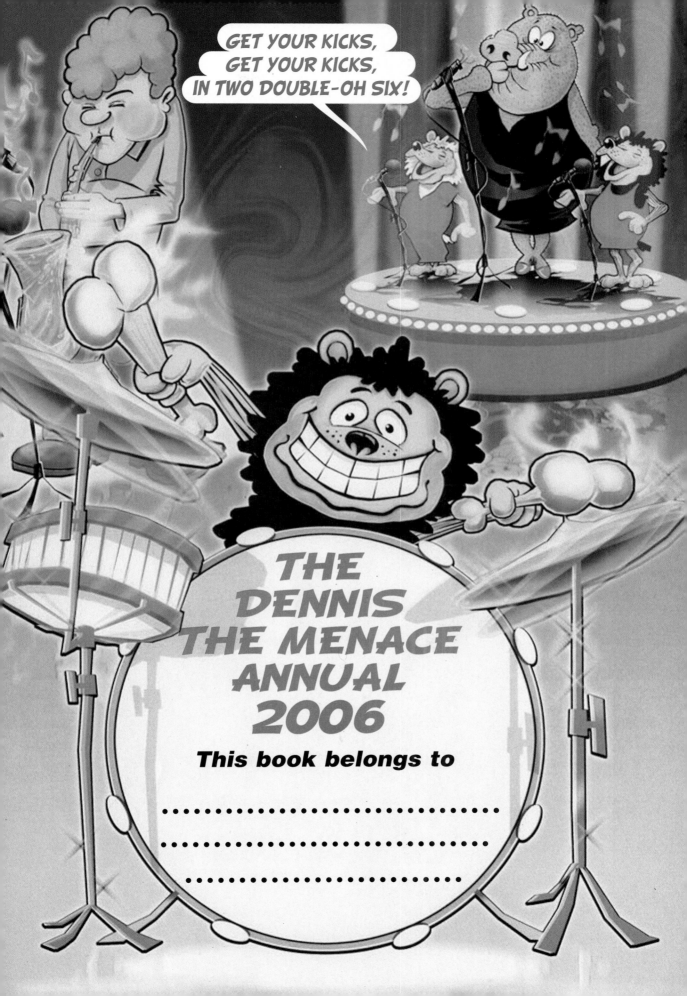

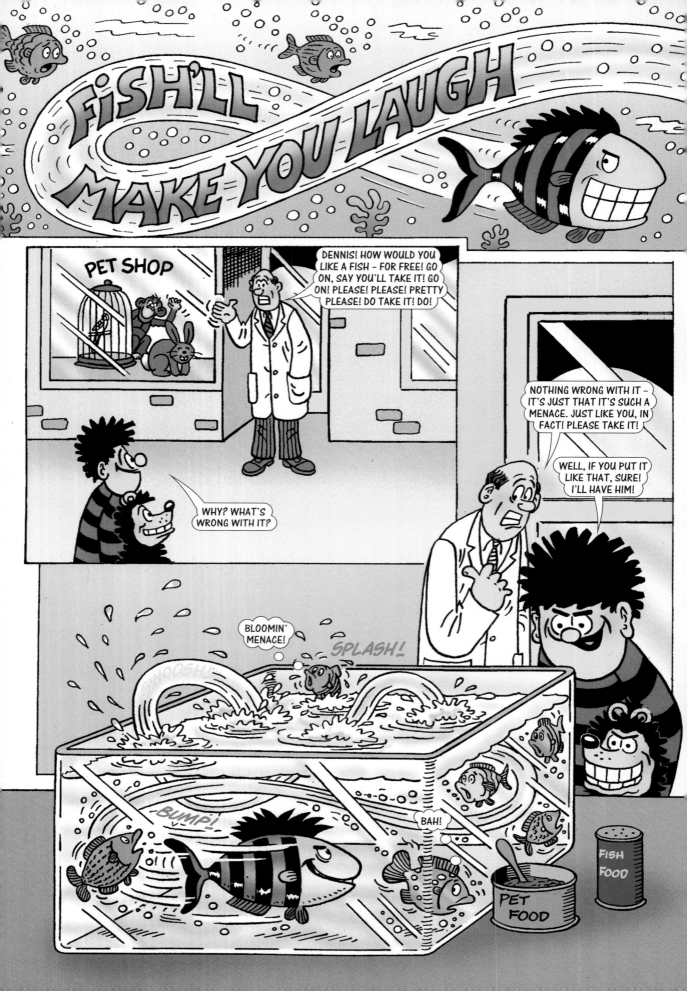

RULED THE EARTH!

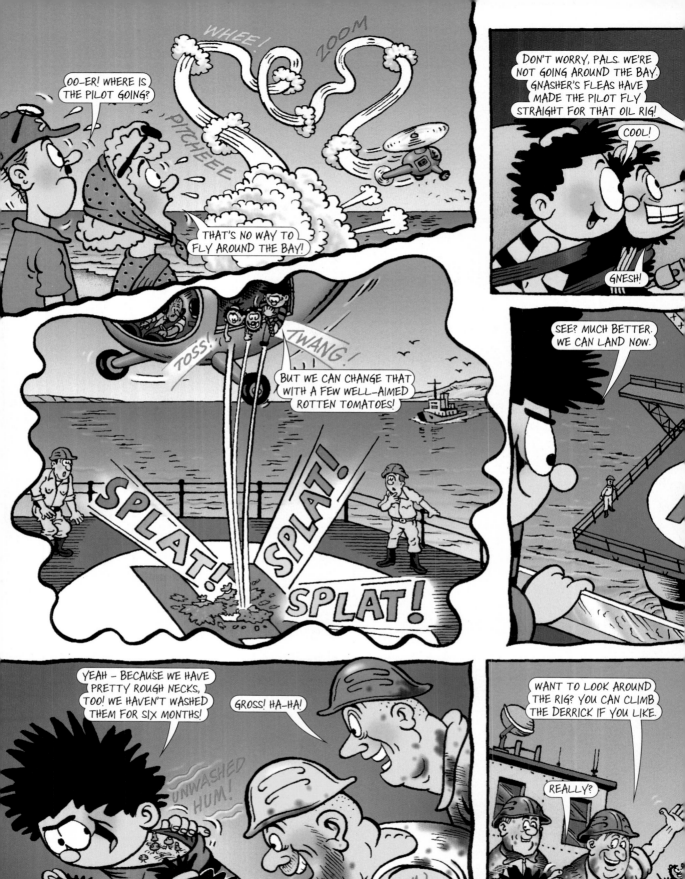

WOW! GREAT FEED!

BURP!

I'M STUFFED!

BUT WE CAN'T LAND ON THE RIG YET. IT'S NOT READY.

HIYA, GUYS!

JUMP!

MENACES! NICE TO HAVE YOU ON OUR RIG! WE'RE ROUGHNECKS!

ROUGHNECKS? THAT'S WHAT YOU GUYS ARE KNOWN AS.

FUNNY, 'AT!

VERY UNDERSTANDIN' OF 'IM!

DEREK

YOU'RE A NICE LAD, DEREK, FOR LETTIN' ME CLIMB YA!

TWIST! SQUEEZE!

DEREK

SILLY BEA! THE DERRICK IS THE TALL BIT ON THE RIG! I'M DEREK!

SCREECH!

So –

A VISIT TO THE THEATRE IS SUCH A GNICE TREAT FOR US!

WHERE CAN WE SIT?

ONLY THE BEST SEATS FOR US! COOL PLAY, EH?

SURE IS! WANT SOME POPCORN, PALS?

POPCORN

POPCORN

I SAY!

COMMON AS MUCK!

GOTTA BE SAUSAGES! LOTS OF 'EM! A BIG PILE OF SIZZLING SOZZYS, PLEASE!

SIR! THIS IS THE RITZ! WE DO NOT SERVE SAUSAGES!

SAUSAGES? SO CRUDE!

DONK!

BARRY GLENNARD

BAH! IT'S NO TREAT FOR US!

WAHEY!

YIPPEE!

GNALTON TOWERS

THE BIG-DIPPER

AFTER ALL THAT, WE'RE EXHAUSTED!

YEAH! TIME TO TREAT OURSELVES TO ....

HOW UNCOUTH!

Next –

DINNER AFTER THE THEATRE IS SUCH A TREAT. PICK ANYTHING YOU WANT, GNIPPER!

DON'T MIND IF I DO, DAD! WHAT WILL I HAVE?

EEK!

SHRIEK!

GNO WORRIES! WE'LL JUST TAKE OUR CUSTOM ELSEWHERE!

SEE YA!

Later –

CANDY FLOSS

I'D LIKE TO TREAT MYSELF TO – EVERYTHING YOU'VE GOT!

WOW! WHAT A TREAT IT WOULD BE TO RIDE THAT!

BEANOTOWN BEAUTY SALON

... A BIT OF PAMPERING!

SO RELAXING!

BAH! YOUR TOUGH CLAWS HAVE MANGLED OUR FILES!

MINCED OUR CLIPPERS!

TIME WE WERE OFF, ANYWAY!

BACK TO THE SUPERMARKET.

ZIP!

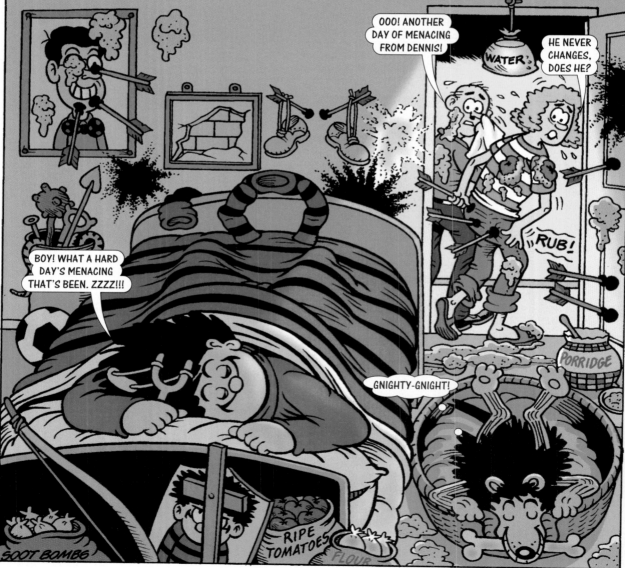

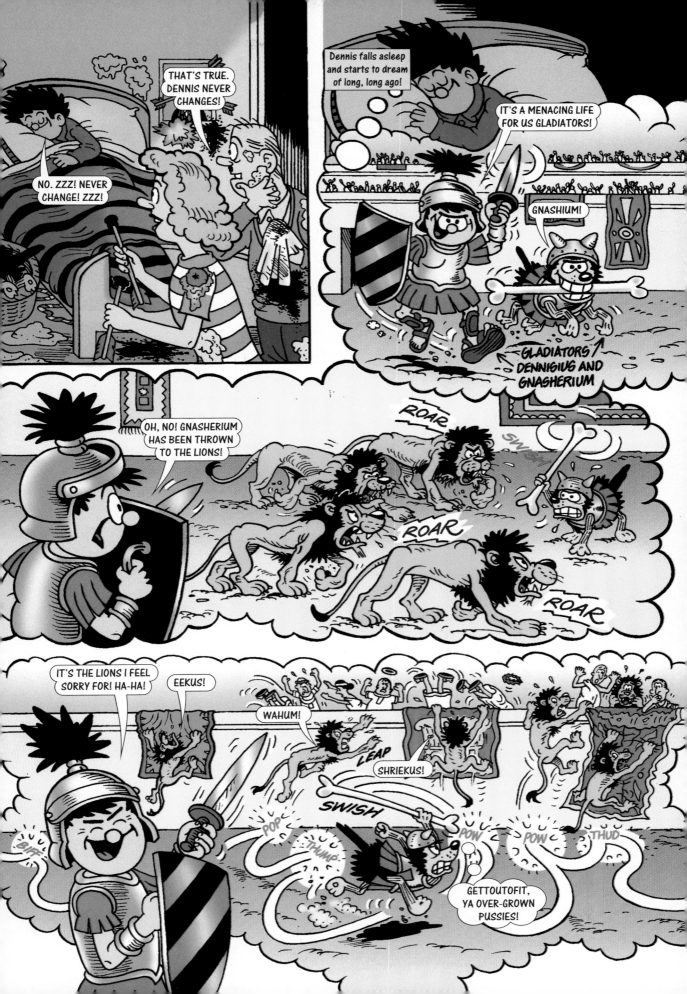

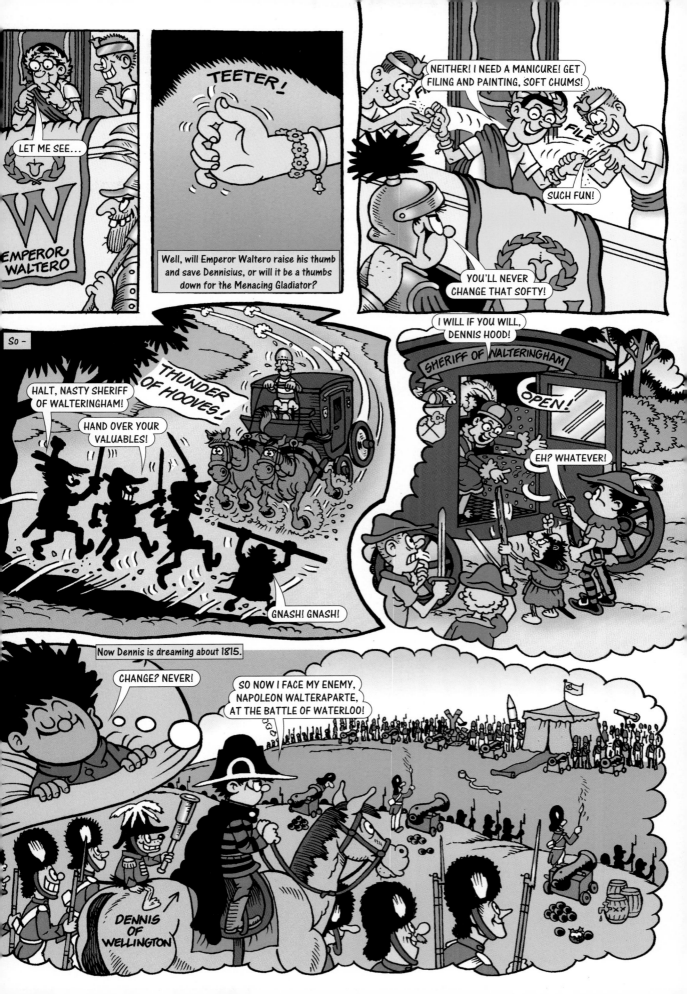

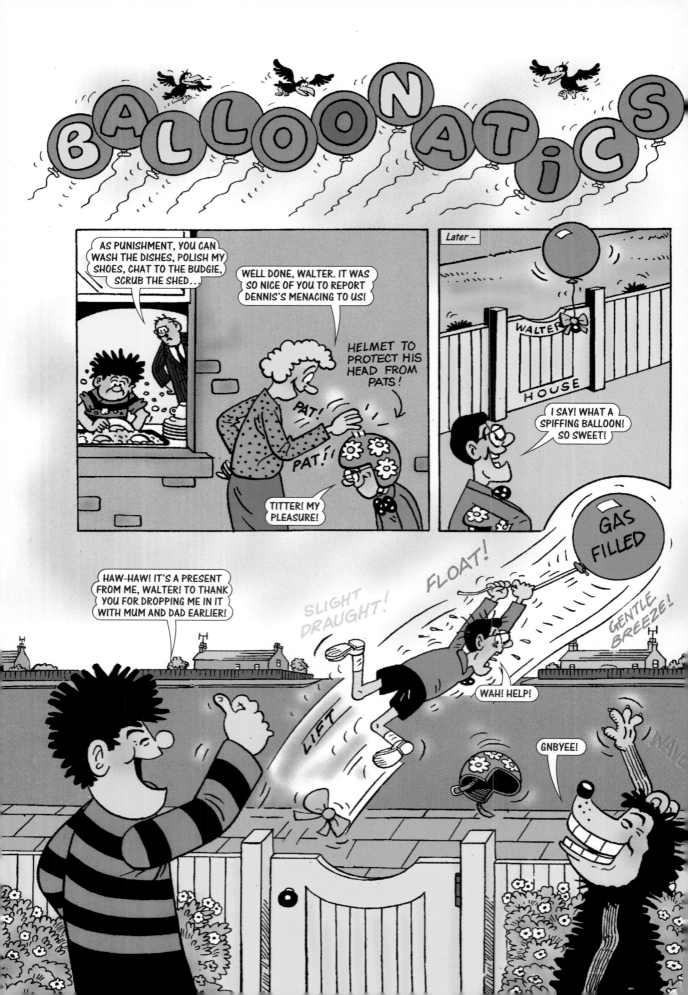

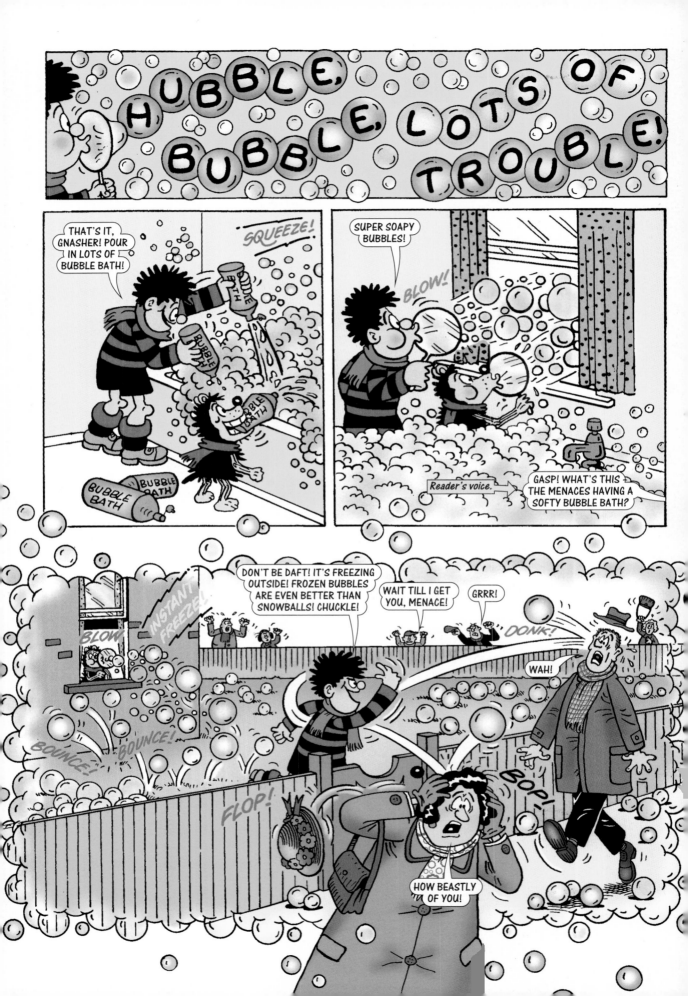

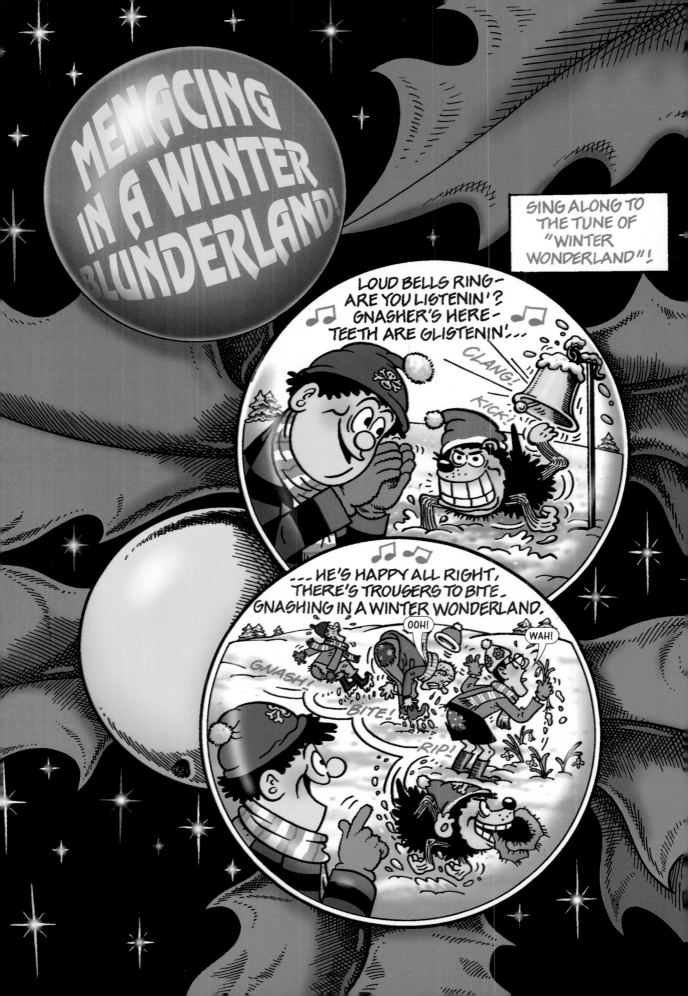